Forgotten Works
Collected Poems
1987-1992

Charles Blackwell

I would like to especially mention my wife Meredith, who supported
the idea of sharing these poems and has tolerated my efforts at
editing.
Also, to my son Charles IV who was the inspiration for some of
these poems and has grown into a remarkable young man.
To my granddaughters Elizabeth and Scarlett who will hopefully
read and maybe understand this work someday.

Published by: Blackwell

ISBN: 979-8-9988469-2-2   e-book
         979-8-9988469-4-6   Hardcover
         979-8-9988469-3-9   Paperback

Table of Contents:

God's Gift

I stood before the moon and called your name:

God's gift, beauty thing

And the night fog closed in

Heavy it breathed and the moon hung there

a pearl now, alabaster, thin veined and blue beneath thick areola.

The womb world opened to welcome young love lost, us perfected.

Waiting to be reborn beneath soft silk baby's hair

and warm enfolding closeness.

A welcoming tongue's cross, push, caress, taste of teeth and lips

and lids of bluest morning eyes that love

and hold and speak hush whispered breath raw and tight.

Arms and fingers that hold, squeeze, scratch into me,

into you, breath leaves hot sweat and thighs

pull in sweet release and ecstasy

Tossed hair and eyes that look, me, and hold, me

and thank

Your Face

Your face: neither beautiful nor ugly,

but right, too right, to me.

Your eyes a strong secret hidden to be held,

deepening blue tenders, fragile

sadness amid lighter frames, support of bone.

To dream of hair too fine,

to feel it lay against my throat at night,

a long night.

Emotions pure and light as your flesh.

These things my hated friend at night, alone.

You do not know your secret.

The story of bones close to surface,

where you say yes, and no with voice uncertain,

eyes forcing no more questions,

beneath brow that has said your answer,

has told your story

and waits for you to live it.

My Eyes

My eyes, you say, they hold you
Whisper, whisper dreams, saying it softly
Small fingers flowing through my hair
And touching me please, on the brow, cheek, lips
Fingers soft, words soft, breath soft to caressing
Feeling scent, knowing the alive fresh and
The pulling stroking gentle ease from hiding
Of the scared parts of me.
Wanting now, only wanting, in eyes
Ready to tear as soft gentles welcome and
Once alone am now there with, and you touch me
Running waters of sorrow, of welcome and thanks
Salt fresh and tongue stale of lips alive and
You to hold me.
The hand on neck, on chest,
The mouth-loving shape of caressing hellos
And I want yous, and the need
Need for even a me as your arms move from
Shoulders to hold, come closer, to be with me
Now you want and let my eyes close
To yours closed with warm softs of scent
Tastes of texture warm with tights of breathing
Your breathing next to me, alive
Warming me as holding

It could come as images

It could come as images
flashes of feeling that lead me to turn,
looking for you. Maybe I'm driving
and remember with a suddenness
that pulls my breath tight.
The whisper of what once was a sob,
and I know that I'm not driving to you.

I hold her. Her hand in mine is smaller,
I squeeze lightly to be sure.
Sometimes I kiss her and my eyes,
They open again just to be sure that it is not you.
Though her lips taste smaller
and teeth feel tighter, more her.
Sometimes I breathe her scent,
remembering something new, not mine.

There are these times when I make,
I must make new paths through memory.
When I still feel you close to me
and must block the push of emotions,
The promises, futures, the love talk.
The only way I have, to stop now,
is by the losing of you and
the replacement with this thing,
this betraying monster who lied,

and hurt herself and me, and our family,
our futures, our pasts.

All paths get blocked eventually.
The new kissing remembrances are
led through other parts,
the feel of holding gets routed through new.
She's no less for not being five years my partner.
Carefully her voice is laid in the new,
Her feel in the fresh.
I start to build the enclosing of the past,
And carefully begin an impossible.

When you really love

When you really love someone.
When it's cold you let them climb naked
beneath the blankets
to settle against your warmth and flannels.
You kiss their ears wet from the shower,
let their hair lay cold on your shoulder,
feel their goose-pimpled legs against your thighs
take their icy feet between yours, toast them,
let your arms be pulled around them like extra blankets,
 feel cold nipples as the lungs lift and lower the chest,
feel the shiver and be surprised when they turn to kiss you with
tight cold lips,
just how hot
their tongue is.

I have replaced you

I have replaced you, my love, with another.

Her hair is not so soft and her skin not as accepting of my touch.

But her eyes can hold mine nearly as yours.

Her breath is unfelt against me as I sleep

but I know, secure, that she is there.

This love is not as strong as our first love.

This love can still make me cry,

at night, alone, without her.

She is not as beautiful except in a dark perfect way.

I use her love as I would not use yours,

to fill the empty hollows where love should be.

Filling me, she cushions the broken parts

so, they do not rattle as I walk, alone.

This love is better than no love at all.

Barely

I look in a mirror

I look in the mirror and stare surprised
to find, not you, but myself there.
Who have I been talking to?

I cannot hide from you,
always in my thoughts.
My leg, your arm, a dream,
whose dream, whose body.

In your dream I kill me.
Why would I hurt him?
What did he do?

Do I fear the pain of
confronting a mistake.
Scape goat, lily worm,
roach motel of curses.
I will live in you and kill him.

I used to believe

I used to believe your eyes when you said you loved me.

I used to cry when you said we would be

together, forever, in love.

I used to laugh and hold your hand.

I used to sleep with you in my arms.

And I used to dream of you and me.

I used to believe.

Lies

Your skin is so soft

But it's not, it's grainy.

It's been tanned too many times,

your cheek has fuzz like your belly.

Your eyes, such eyes, I can look into them forever.

Maybe for a long time anyway

Because then I'm sure you're looking at me.

I know it's me when you sigh

I'm not trying to seduce you

Believe me, it's okay

I don't think I love you

But will you smile if I do?

can I stay the night or week,

will you love me?

I like your laugh,

It's so authentic

or real, anyway,

when you look at me.

Your lips, so tasty, yum

that makes it easy to kiss you,

 so easy, so warm, so wet, enfolding.

I love the way you hum and purr,

and pant, when I kiss your neck

lick your ears, trace your shoulder

and chest, first button, second.

Your hair doesn't bother me.

It's dry. Well, like hair in my mouth.

Better when it's salty with sweat

I like it when you run your fingers through my hair

warm flowing expression of relaxing caress

till I'm trapped where you like me to be.

I found you

I found you without believing it
maybe without you ever believing it.
But I found you in the emptiness
before we forgot we made each other whole.
When I'm scared, really scared, or alone
your voice gentles me. When I took your hand
and gave you mine, they fit together perfect
a miracle. Maybe, just maybe
what we laughed about once
when young, the circles, following ourselves
leading to each other, the circles
Circles round again and we laughed.
Your eyes took mine then
and we let them go free
and they held to each other.
Circles. Even now, if you let it,
quieted the voices in your head,
the thought of hurt or right.
Your eyes would circle to mine,
compasses knowing what we fear most.

There was

There was what?
Let's say five months
And we talked

Often, maybe more
Than just often
On a phone whose
Warm plastic feel
Couldn't replace you
Soft, tickling, whispers
Your hair to fall
Across my face
Hand on my arm

Leaning, there was always
Leaning between us

Couldn't walk into a room
And resist the urging
The not-so-subtle tugs
That pull me to you

I could lay down
With your voice
Pillows, blankets, and sleep
It gave me a purring

Offer my throat for
The soft stroking
Of your voice
Your legs to intertwine with mine
I could slide my head
Under your chin

And now?
There is the phone
To hold in plastic the
Memory of your voice
There are dreams
The wonderful aching
Of a need to feel you
Close and closer

You are warm and
Put your arms around me
Putting mine around you
The distance to fall
Following your eyes
Reaching towards you

With the feeling

I wake with the feeling

Of her hand

Under mine

On the pillow

Feeling her fingers

Stroke hair behind my ears

Touching me solely because

It's the feel of me

She loves and hums

The taste of my teeth

She hungers for

My weight to bear

Her down as requested

Loves to be held

Fresh showered skin

Touching and heat mingling

We stick and she slides

You look

God, you look beautiful, your shape is yum

flesh on flesh like this I could hold you

just watching you purr and scratch finely

I'm glad I can make you smile

and Oh God, bite your lip

and roll like animals with me

But's it's your eyes that lock me

keep me when they see me

It was great, of course I enjoyed it

But did you

    now that we lie sweat stuck and panting

did you? Did you really

It's fine if you just want to lie

here curled against me

nesting into my arm you hold

a new teddy bear who feels your heart

as it slows, and quiets

We can lie here of course

I can watch you sleep

your hair in my mouth

some parts sore

Fuzzies

We spent those years huddled close as animals.

The scared hiding behind the frightened.

Cut off from a normal life of study

or play we worked and got by.

Around us, in the hollows grew a rich half life

Of fuzzies chasing sparkling lies,

"Yeeking" over dreadful "gookies".

We nuzzled as hedgehogs do

slithered as snakes and came together

as kittens in heat.

Our world turned upon a thought:

Forever and always, we were.

Fuzzy bones

I've been loving you in the moonlight

Asleep, I wake in a tangle of arms and legs

Not knowing where I end, and you begin.

Making love, I look in your eyes, so they hold me.

You have a sound of frustrated pleasure

That changes to relief and sometimes

I look at your face flushed; your eyes closed

As you hug yourself and thank me, and

God, And oh yes, and my name

My name so loud, your eyes open

And I want to die, just at that moment

To become light and shining.

Heaven

On my lap popcorn,
popped in a pot, smothered in melted butter
We eat and drink iced tea
Heaven smells of you and popcorn
Fingers like this, thin, small nails translucent, strong
and chin shaped like yours alone
with your lips catching popcorn from your hand
pulling them in between teeth, so familiar, they taste like
Your eyes, your eyes are clear, and defined
and in the centers, I fall beyond them,
and into you and live
  You're wearing my shirt, or I thought it was mine
  I hold your hand not busy with popcorn or
  do you hold mine. It's yours, I remember
  this one has your ring, and you watch tv and talk and
  never notice that I look at you, your face,
  breathe in your scent and feel you in my hand
  not knowing until you turn and catch me
"Nothing"
    "Is something wrong, do I have popcorn on my face?"
"You're staring, what's wrong?"
"Nothing, you're just beautiful"
"Thank you, I think"
"I like looking at you"
"But you make me nervous"

19

"Can I kiss you?", "yes"
Something happens as our lips touch
I am living. Your eyes are open,
watching me kiss you, both lips,
then one, then two, bottom, top, caress of tongue, playful
then sweet, and your eyes close
With me inside them and you kiss me
one lip, tongue, mouth open, my teeth, your teeth
taste of butter and you my mouth, your tongue
I taste you and your hand closes on mine tighter
Then a touch, hot, sticky, two fingers on my cheek
Tracing, then my neck, and then you hold
my head and kiss me
My hand moves to your waist
fabric, skin, ribs above and hips below
tummy waist, warm, you 're sweating
I am too
And this moment doesn't stop
Your hand, my hand we hold, we kiss, we live
 in love everything is right

Twenty days

In twenty days, you pulled me close
sitting on my chest said "Fuck me "
I rolled you over and kissed your ear,
bit it laughing uh-huh, said let' s "woogie!"
You slid my shorts down with a hand
and a foot saying "Yeek" and giggled
as I kissed your eyes hair, cheek, neck and chin.
Tasted your lips pulled away
compressing your thighs between mine
slid chest and belly teasing
to taste your neck, then shoulders,
fingers in my hair, kissing, held my throat
I licked and swallowed as your chest rose,
my hair brushing your breast
then the other as I nuzzled,
you held me to your swollen breast,
it leaked against my chin
and sighing you said "it's been forever", hugging me.
I said, "I love you", and breathed
against your wet hand.
You wriggled as I lay on your thighs
saying to me "please"
I pulled you close and sweating met your lips,
your heart beat your nipples hard
against my chest for a moment,
then sliding your legs,

kissed again and sucking your lip,

opened my teeth to your tongue.

I felt your hand slide between

our bellies where you still bulged

and along your scar

scratching me with your stubble,

then kissing me, your small fingers tried

to pull me in just a bit

your breath caught and

feeling your thighs push mine apart

I pulled back and you pulled me in

again and said "please", grabbing my ass,

your teeth pressed on my shoulder and neck,

second by second you pulled my life into yours,

gliding while licking, pressing your thighs

beneath mine in another second

your hands around my waist

pulling, I feel you slide and

moving squeezing, a sudden "ouch"

and I freeze, about to lick your ear.

"No?" I whisper. But, shimmying your legs free

you say "yes" and "I don't care"

as the minutes catch up and

your legs encircle me, filling me

with your breaths and

humming as I feel fully,

and my hair meets your stubble

your YES as I ease back the seconds

gently slide up to us the minutes

I feel the days as at 18, mother and father,

we fill, and empty, and breathe each other and

I come to love your stretch marks

as much as your tears

when you try to say you love me,

when you hold our son and I hold you.

But it's not that, now, in bed you hum and

growl and roll me over to hide our faces

beneath your hair and you knead my chest

as I read the stories in your stretch marked hips

then tease your back till you squeeze down

on me and say,

"Don't move, don't you ever move."

PLEASE

kiss the sweat in my hair

let my tears fall on your neck

hold me like this

smooth my shaking

whisper my name in my ear

as I try to open my eyes

to find you nowhere near

Come lick my chin

Oh, come lick my chin and ear
finger my face in the dark
let me kiss your wrist free of its scars
hold your pain to my chest

Pink Highlighter

I found this notecard first on the kitchen table

in our tiny first apartment a few years ago.

It showed up today, behind some socks in your drawer.

A drawer not opened since you left.

Happy writing in pink highlighter

     "See you later, I love you

              Dorothy "

this notecard, a filed image leading my heart

to an apartment lawn, to dance in lovely sweat,

and sweet flesh heat with you on a warm spring night beneath

a thousand stars overhead

with loving tired kisses stored for now.

I search to pull out from the dust

Memories once put there fearing this day

     Your hand in mine

     closing fingers tight

     I dumbly smile as your hair tickles my belly.

     You smile as you slide your body up mine

     to tell me you love me

     crafty smile as you lay your breasts on me.

     Seductive as your seriousness brings me to heaven.

     Then you doubt your effect, laugh and

     you say, swinging breasts

"Get naked Big Boy"
and I do

Notecards fall into place.

I reach for the filing drawer to pull myself up
And over to blessedly, unthinkingly, fly
To land amongst more friendly memories

The drawer is full of me and you, and tumbling us.
A heavy white sheet gets draped over the too well known,
Familiar features, now best left unseen.
A hand, long fingered and pale
Grasps the edge of the drawer
Not pulling towards, but pushing away from
The white ceramic tiled room and you
Colder than me now being filed too.

Pretty girl

Nice girl, pretty girl

Sweet girl

What is it your father whispers

In your ear now?

You told me he wanted a boy

You who climbed trees and

Scraped your knees bloody.

Hated the dresses

What will you do for him now?

Young, anorexic with hatred for

Every hint of your womanly figure.

You raced to win for him

Jumped your hurdles until your knee

Went purple and you called the other girls

Sugar cubes for not running in the rain.

Your dad was a stranger to you.

Always stuck at work, only hints of him.

He liked your sister more, you complained.

She was smarter, prettier and everyone's favorite.

Hating her as much as wanting to be her,

You were torn apart trying to be her.

When your cousins lived with you,

One stole your things and the other

Stole touches in the back of the car.

Mom was a drunk, you said, hating her.

She called you a slut for dating,

Reminding you that your dad wanted a boy

While hitting you and screaming.

Then you grow too tall, too big and

She hugged you so you couldn't breathe

Reminding you that your sister was better still.

You told me your dad did not care about anything.

Did not care about your mom's boyfriends or

How you cried when she introduced you to

The one hiding drunkenly in the garage after school.

So, you were always hiding, always sick over

Your mom's smoking and the allergies, weak.

Did you choose marriage to escape that?

Was I your doorway out, to being loved?

Once you escape, you quit coughing,

You ate and got healthy, no longer bruising

Fragile skin over knees, elbows and hips.

You were proud of your curves.

Now the creative one who was tough yet warm,

Loved and soon you believed it too as you grew.

Now you could cut out your mother.

You got attention from your father as

You became his smart, pretty one.

The only daughter left within his reach.

An escape from his drunken burden and

His tiny computers and toys.

Now he had always wanted you,

Now you were his best child,

The one with the grandchild for him.

Now he had a family worth retiring for, being home.

You have always been beautiful now,

always smart, always wanted.

Now you can have anything

Even to be the lost daughter returning

Now your dad has always loved you

Your mom has always loved you

Your sister now envied you

Aren't you the perfect sweet girl?

Babies slept

I once believed that newborn babies
slept through the night.
At 2 a.m. though, I learned
much to my tired wife's delight
that hungry babies know there is only
the now and forever.
I know that babies require a lot of love and patience.
A smile during the toxic diaper changes.
A million small catches as they walked from Mom to me,
smiled and fell, and bumped, and smiled still.
Padded bottomed adventurers.
I want to believe that I will always catch him,
protected as he moves from you to me.
Child, forever.

Son

Do you remember our two cats?
Did I tell you how Mike cried
When Ike got hit in the road?
That night as I buried him,
Mike sniffed and walked around
and made this sound.
The same sound he'd make when
They accidentally got shut in separate rooms.
That night he made it again, and Ike lay asleep
dead and I cried.
Wet fur, he was still not there.
And well, Oh God.
I heard that noise again tonight.
That crying sound only Mike can make.
And you see now.
Mommy got you.
And I got support bills.
And you're not here.
And she's not either.
And Mike was on my lap
and he was wet and purring
under my hand. And it was me
making that sound.

Heaven for Charlie

You are with me
we laugh and hold hands
sitting on a couch
Our couch in our apartment
with our son
A room away and quiet
We said our "night-night, I love you.
Dream of bunny rabbits and transformers,
of little bear and everything sweet."
Asleep on his bed, a mattress on the floor
with blankets and pillows, bears and rabbits.
Standing there to turn off the light
I remembered the monsters
under the bed
that almost got me,
But you're safe

Busting

Son, where you can still laugh

and in my memories:

"Bust those ghosts"

"Daddy", you say "get the trap,

Quick, Quicker, NOW!"

and you stomp the trap and smile.

You want to help me build things.

Hit a nail fifty times and it barely moves.

Yet you put on your 'seat belt' of my tools

and try to fix things still.

I smile, inside, to see your mother's smile,

her eyes next to yours and

her laugh as she hugs you.

You carry my tools, but with them

I couldn't fix what was broken.

You try, so honest in effort. You try.

For you and your mom

I would have done anything,

I did everything I could.

Yet we're broken still.

You can hit a nail fifty times

and still laugh.

When

When God? The only question comes
for you to be, simply be.
Then I no longer beg nor ask for help
doing better now, at least worthy of you,
the world is made of the wall before me,
carpet beneath knees, over floor
yet darkness now has more walls, doors,
and there are not just voices calling
nor mouths biting, hiding from pain and tears,
very, very alone tears.
When the brain settles,
nestles loving into cold fluid
in pan of skull and nerves connect feeling to knowing
becomes as it works from here to there
receiving signals of what is, must be,
that can exist in the dark behind lights
or are only walls, walls,
small moving molecules to make all this,
not dreams nor words that spell
to create what holding wants to be.
When truth settles over truth
Real hides dreams
wants of real fighting the real
until arguing demands hurt brain
once more and begging God to be,

to maybe just be,
listen if not to act,
but to fill spaces I can't,
to protect and build guidance of
light over loved ones
but my ineffectualness
towards them hides my failures with
God being and to maybe not condemn me.
Then thoughts come,
feelings go about one another,
past each other, moving
and forgetting that I am
and think of doing for me what is needed,
more than others want.
But not quite there
until confusion moves and hides me
from not being which brings pain
equal to my needs
I want the doing,
not crying or tears
want more of all
and less of some
and just to be, please.

Even I don't like me

Even I don't like me mostly dead now
In tighter circles my blood journeys
Keeping me alive

No urge to move, to warm my extremities,
To flow to the dangerous outer parts

Even a pipe opening wouldn't
Be felt in this drought

Those paths are shunned
Riverbeds clogged by flood wash debris
Closed trading paths to bankrupt wastelands

Unfriendly input is given over again
The world shuns this unalive white flesh
A Ghost chill passing with the touch
It slows, energy is lost
Given over to settling
To sinking.

There's a weird

Theres' a weird obsession I have

Or cultivated, hold dear and dread

Maybe it's a dream or a promise

Induced by delirium through depression

And still, I'm afraid to voice it

To pronounce it in prophet fashion

The women to complete the circle

Ten partners of all types to finish it:

Childhood friend, and the cheerleader

The stranger, the voice from far away

The endowed one still young

A crazy rich engineer

Someone small chested and daring

Someone large, someone older

Now only that one left and I will know

If it's truth or a lie

Will it go full circle to the

Impossible beginning or

Will I be set free?

Maybe end short?

I'm confused by my certainty

Sweet

Perhaps I call your name in the night
to hear only your name, if not you breathing,
slightly snoring next to me.
And the light of streetlamps does not
shine through bedroom blinds to paint
nose and chin and length of hair
in lamp pink of made moons.
But I may feel your leg against my knee
as I shy closer, feel satin over perfect skin
of shoulder, a whisper movement and smiling
you snuggle closer.
Familiar bones and softs relax and breathe
and rub chin into my hand, to take it
as a bear or blanket,
as a hiding nesting place.
Amidst family scents of breath,
female sweat and happy wets
you pull me closer, I am your husband,
your mate with the promise of loving
rolling about my ears, in hollows echoing,
the scream of your name begins
as your scent disappears,
your touch is cold before my hand,
and opening eyes see only empty pillow
and bare walls that mirror terror
in eyes that see terror in themselves

and the scream does not mercifully die
but rises to waken neighbors as world spins
about a pillow and anchor of you is lost.

Cannot sleep

When I cannot sleep because the walls whisper your name

And when holding your pillow to breathe your scent

doesn't help anymore

I just go sleep on the couch

Sometimes, in that empty apartment you left me

You are everywhere now because you are not

And I beg for you

When begging becomes crying

and the walls breathe you back to me faster,

the bed, the couch, the kitchen, the bathroom,

our son's room, all empty

I learned to scream quietly

I've learned to take bad news better

It doesn't ruin my whole day except that

Sometimes when I laugh at things that aren't funny.

Like when our son tells me that mommy cried

Because her boyfriend broke up with her.

Stupid things are funny but to stop laughing

I hit something, dent a wall so the hurt helps me

cry again and not laugh.

The tricks are not easy ones.

I learned to eat my body from inside.

Burning great holes with stomach acid

and after that I'm not crying about you anymore.

Silence has a buzz

Silence has a buzz like alone has fear.

Closed eyes have ghosts when squeezed into hiding.

Breath comes as heartbeats counted now in the rocking postures of knowing.

I want to sing something my mother taught before my eyes found her.

From when god was blond and skies were his eyes and

sleeping was his breast.

When the world spoke and I only knowing thump-thump and

something new; a just learned cold,

the exploding in here of open eyes,

the fighting through this, this space connecting me to warm and soft,

now pain.

But I was, and it was.

Was, I knew when I heard your voice,

your touch already familiar,

and you tasted as warm as your scent soft.

To feel your smile on me was to again recognize god.

Seeing for beginning that mouth full of breast, warm soft,

quiet thump-thumps caressing was not a me thing.

Was, was a caring for me thing. And I dreamed then

knowing hearing of my last thump-thump

was from your wrinkled

soft chest holding my…

where noise comes

and your scent to say…

But I was gone.

Death can rise in you

Death can rise in you.

If you have it, you hold it there,

black and comforting, a pearl.

Deep inside you hold it,

and show it to yourself.

At night, in the hollowness,

It rolls loose among memories.

The crashing, falling sounds, a lost feeling of love.

You can hold it in your hand and finger it numbly about.

You would expect it to be heavier.

It can sink through the skin.

Into the veins where you cut at it.

Awash in your blood, it rolls.

The veins you open before it.

It reaches your heart.

It is now hate, and it will crush.

Growing still, your lungs quit.

Your eyes skitter for a tool,

Something to open your life,

To scrape the hate out.

It was never for attention.

This time is for compassion.

This time is not for pain.

This time it is done.

weakly, quietly

You

You said, you loved

bleeding. Twisting, turning, spinning, cutting,

Impact. Run down halls screaming.

Bruise, crash, break, hurt.

Twist, turn, spin, cut, Bleed.

Yes, I will, I promise. Love me.

Live for us, live for you.

Bigger Than me.

Part of a whole.

I can never leave you.

Forever. Just please love me: It was you.

Til death do us part. Make it yours.

It is mine, please love me.

I can't stop loving you.

You are my Life.

Statement, truth, life.

I am yours, don't hurt me.

Uncaring, you kill me.

A promise

To you, to me, to everything.

Til death do us part.

Cold comfort.

I already gave my life.

To just hang on hoping.

Once I was begged

Once I was begged to say mine
To be an us, with an ours, together
And your body welcomed mine
Told itself to me with indrawn breaths
Eyes closed, and a pressing together
To say itself in me.
But a we was withdrawn, you took the ours,
Pain was a no, a me not you.
Only a tear could be shed amongst the blood,
The draining of one from the other,
A separating of lives.

The images

The images are all thumbed cards
maybe lifted, replaced,
sorted in fields sweeping
deliberate movements to push gods
recall names for emotions,
for dreams of brown
hair replacing blond
for her face over yours
thumbing down
I am reminded of the price
already paid for a chance at love
the love that, oh gods, I begged for.
And you, I realize, are the canvas,
no, the land my dreams grew from.
You're the name I've given to love
the other half of my soul
What God gave in return for my dreams
the thumbed cards are only cards
I rub clean the stars, the night
the universe I lean on, I made
and now try to build a card house in.
Try to forget that it's only my one small house
in a great big world.

Nobody

Jawing the words in the midnight surround

Want, wanting to speak or to have

To feel and hold, slip inside

And explode into being.

Not quite, shake head and work jaw

It creaks like worn floorboards

Before the door I squeeze eyes

The closing in of light pressed hard

Head into hands, the rise and crashing

Noises onto my shoulders, unseen

Felt though, felt like an urge to breathe

As dirt tossed onto my grave

Those things that exist

Those things that are not me

They fall in and are not

But I am alone as before birth

Knowing now that in the life around

Nobody is holding me

At night

I dream about it at night

Hold it on my tongue like honey.

A promise of an end, and I fear it.

It makes me stupid as I stare and now am lusting for it.

Taking my sight, my world, my life into it.

Promises, pain, future in stone.

Solid, heavy, slow truth.

They come, angels, demons,

powers of nature, my Gods.

They argue and gamble for my bones,

worn, useless, weak and brittle now.

Yet I call, and feed the night my fear, and love.

Suffering so delicate it does not fill their empty bellies.

But they are held still, drawn to my blood I hold forth,

Communion to spirits and promises.

My dark horde of memories and love.

Come, take, drink, this is my life which I shed for thee,

that there might be forgiveness of me.

For thine is the power, the hope, the glory.

So, saying, I empty what could be into what was.

Tasting what is. Poison, slow spreading,

sickly sweet and noxious.

In fear I welcome it.

That hurt

Do you know that hurt?
How sweet it feels when all I can do
Is hug me and say "no"
when it's like a tooth nerve shining into my skull
Feeling like a scraped knuckle, a stubbed toe
Pulling me away from the holding to lick and
Tongue and suck what hurts,
Murmuring to the bleeding that pulls
Drowning air from my ears
I grabbed something I cannot let go of
Soul tied to what was pushed over to sink.
Wriggling into darkness rushing past in descent
Shiver and try to pull that weight back up
But it pulls me down more.
I hold onto it now as if it was you.
Grey light above fading, so cold I'm blessed
By waters pushing into my chest that aches, numbing it
Below is darkness pulling

Last prayer

Someone should pity the victims of suicide:
The jilting lover, the unfaithful wife,
The murderer who takes all of a family, but one.

Hold them as they cry or laugh now
In astonishment "it wasn't my fault."
Because they are correct.

Nobody can return love as it is given.
Vows are not meant to be kept
Your life is not your family

The suicide forces it on you
Raises the guilt of shame
Shines on you the light of broken faith
Or the despair of being alone.
It is a crime they do

Protect the victim at night,
in another's arms as just
Before sleep they hear the heartbeat of the gone.
Sounding alive, in the body they now hold.

Don't you understand

But don't you understand
It hurts
Truly, lord almighty hurts
Without you it hurts
I couldn't breathe or walk
I tried my own arms to hold me
But the feeling choked and burnt.
Your noise exhaled from the walls
Your prints stuck to the sheets
My fingers tasted notes you had written
And finally, I believed your assurances
I wasn't good enough to be
I tongued each curse and agreed
I was bad, should go away, we hated me

Where I can hide

Where can I hide from the terrible shades of your love.

Amongst those broken things called memories.

There is a dark around living light.

A me holding you.

An Our hands.

A Your lips to mine.

Wandering lost.

So many signs to ways now gone.

Wandering lost

to you no more.

They hear the grief of my scream,

  the laugh of my frustration they know.

  They will not look where my eyes lead,

  to me lost, wandering and forget the safe,

  the here I came in,

  the not you loving me.

Better

I shouldn't.

The phrase guides.

It hurts me: I shouldn't.

The doctor said so.

I won't.

I shouldn't.

If I wasn't here I would.

But I am, so I won't.

Simple, simplicity, not too hard to do.

Follow what they say.

Do as they say.

I know how to be well.

Even if I am not.

The Lie

It' s never gone.

It's just inside, streaking pain that lies

fires whirling, hell is calling, feral eyes that stare inside

monsters raving, to sand they're stomping

this thing that was I

Green, I hear green mold that's spreading

disease is eating the pain that's crawling

Where am I?

circles, balls are spinning,

flesh is crawling nails to open eyes

See, see, shaking light, fear,

It's hiding as the worm is crawling,

Was it I?

Tears they're falling, hands are wringing

head that's blackened, skin falling from I.

Stomach tensing, muscles wrenching.

 Open, open. close the eye safely hidden,

staring hands that hide

 Pain is driven, darkness calming

lights, streets, town am I

walking slowly, rain is lifting,

scent of growing

love is waiting, thinking I.

 The lie.

It hurts

It hurts
you cry
but just a little.

Cold, almost fear on the ward.
They're crazy, they're here.
They're not leaving, I'm here too.

A cold telephone in the hall carries conversations all night.
The people reach but miss the touch.
Lonely people who are only seen sometimes.
They want to hold something, to let themselves cry.
It hurts, I cannot do that either.
If I open my mouth to scream, I could not stop.
My eyes will hold it in. Here the pain is wrong.
Drug it.

A poem is only of words and fears.
Not plastic sheeted beds and urine-stained chairs,
cold painted block walls, doors that don't lock.
No mentions of plastic knives, plastic bottles,
plastic wrapped food.
Plastic attendants that come and go.

We are different and they know it.

We drag grief to us like blankets in the night.

Or does it attack like flies where we cannot reach.

Something is broken: I cannot remember

the pain or its names or its many faces.

Caress

Sweet, The taste of black bliss on your tongue.

Forgotten, glorified shining idol of grace to be not.

A mouthing babe on bosom.

Milk, life of ending, beginning

Being forever.

Upturned, supplicating receiving.

Eyes rolled behind brows, seeing glory flood thousands,

millions of cells are screaming in pain

and drinking sweet pleasure from emptying

eyes gone marble cold.

Drain, drain.

Hold me as I drain.

Your arms and tears carry me.

My last breath your whispered tear.

CLEANING

Did I tell you about the dreams I forced?
How I lay, eyes tight closed, heart thump throb in my neck.
And there were strands, stray runaways in my mind and straining,
my toes curl tight, and fists clenched.
Breath held and the yellow net I made,
Had always made to drag and fix and clean me.

I dragged out third grade, playing monkeys with friends and then
naked touches and feeling panties against my balls.
How they kissed her and she them and they tasted
like apricot fruit rollups, she said, and you like milk.
And I didn't kiss her, nor touch her, but watched.
They were my only friends then and I dragged watching,
caught the pain of not kissing, of being milky
with guilt over panties and watching, and I cleansed it.

Third grade lived as a six-foot-tall bean plant
 in a glazed dough planter, the size of it all,
of gerbils my teacher gave me and trying to
get friendship I named one someone and he laughed at me.
And I dragged sitting there hearing it and feeling only hurt.

Scoured clean I dragged and had to breathe and my toes
were cramped arcs and you asked me why I can't just love you,
always.
There were things in the way. School, a job

in the mountains and sky, of friends that didn't hurt me,

of pets with their own names. And you were good, so good,

promised so many times that love was forever and

My breath was popping, and my fists shaking, my back arched

to hold my breath as the net pulled

scraping me clean from black top to darker bottom

and it hurt and then I was done.

The air came, dizzy I turned my head aside

thought how stupid I was to drag free everything,

to believe I could clean me of everything but you.

Valentine

You leave me lie in a hospital bed,

Tears rolling across my hand.

Strange blankets hold me.

The hum of ventilators,

Like your breathing,

Brings me sleep.

Years, lifetime.

Lover forever.

A ball, curled.

In sleep fetal

Alone fatal.

Bad, bad

Your defense was the victim.
Always hurt and hurting more
Even when kicking me to bruises
It was only because I had made you hurt.

I made you cry in court, in mediation
The doorstep, the car, everywhere.
You were right, I was bad and had to be hurt.
You shouldn't have loved me. Couldn't have.

I was the weak one, always crying, sad.
You could not have loved me, should not have.
With three months of no job, I was lost to both of us.
I cried, or just sat there staring in emptiness
Too scared to leave the bed, the room, the house.
Scared of reminding you that you could do better.
Scared of being unwanted by you.

When you wanted to suicide yourself, I held you.
Now that I did not sleep for three days, you loathed me.
Without you the apartment howled, we hated me.
I could feel it pulse through me. Promising to only
Get through the day and then the pain could end.

Bad, bad, bad, I was bad

You were right, but please love me
After you left, I begged for your love.
And was told to go die quietly.

What? You were pregnant when you left me?
Why tell me you had to end it because no part of me
Should be allowed to grow in you? Not good enough to live.
I wasn't good enough to live. Not even a lovely little bit of me.

I cried and then bled,
They locked me up to watch me cry all day
They drugged me to keep the blood inside me.
So, I did not cry for two hours.
Then I did not cry for two days.
I could leave by bed, my room, maybe my pain.
Pieces could be pushed back roughly together.
Still not deserving of life.

Jennifer

I thought I heard you scream last night as I lay here.

A voice fully grown up from when you left.

No more the spindly armed, cellophane skinned creature afloat,

taking your life from her life.

You had grown to where your thumb was as large as you when you left.

You had hurt your knee, and it bled redly against your pale, dirty skin.

  Or was it worse? Were you older, caught in the currents of a stream,

  dragged from sight, only a yell 'Daddy' to pull me in after you.

To now search the dark places downstream.

To save you from freezing waters and the fishes and the crabs.

But no, it was stronger, a scream of pain and fear.

You were grabbed on a street, dragged into the dark, beaten

as you screamed louder and louder, so I came running after you,

searching the night, low men to beat off, stinking filth to wipe from you,

to hold you safe once more, a child, my child.

No, the scream was louder, worse. It was of horror and pain.

You were suffering, you were crying, and it would not stop hurting.

You beat at the terrors in the night. Alone and crying you yelled at its

voices, kicked its walls, broke its hands as they grabbed for you.

But it did not stop. You hurt and would not stop hurting.

The pain grew and you sobbed not "Daddy, Daddy."

But "husband, lover, friend".

I tried to find you that night.

Alone in the dark I searched for you,

to hold you from the fears. To pry the razor from your hand,

tie back in your precious blood, life of my love.

And you were not there.

I found you instead inches long, a lump of meat, torn.

I could not bury you nor watch you grow till we ran together, alive.

Yet, you cried still, not knowing why.

Then, blood of my blood, life of my love,

I dove into that stream as a blade cuts into flesh,

searching for the hidden parts until I found them.

And fast at first, then more slowly, so slowly,

drop by timeless drop I came to you.

<u>Trying</u>

I am my skin

my brain grows outside of my skull

my senses are exposed

I see the bugs crawl

about in the grass

feel the bite and brown rub

of dying under the green

these are them

these are them

pictures, thoughts, words

this is

this is

feet nervously bounce against each other

this is,

I'm here.

Block walls

Cold, barren painted concrete block walls, everywhere.

Windows that don't open but let the cold in.

Doors that only unlock to let food pass and doctors in.

No belts, no glass, no sharps, just pain.

In memory the beautiful moments,

a caress, a sigh, a whispered 'I love you'

They float as broken glass in the night.

Cold reflecting images.

They cut. They mutilate.

'til death do us part' the promise.

Warm dripping inside.

A cloying, sticky ooze that silences

the shivers in cold bones:

Warm healing.

The eyes look outward.

Drab sky beyond locked glass.

Frozen earth, dead leaves, square block buildings

 lifeless

There's a string

There's a string of Christmas lights
around the construction of the new Physics lab.
Pretty, dainty against gray concrete,
red steel, and faded men beneath a sweatshirt sky,
dripping sullenly over a campus
spring green and real under the damp sky
and hurrying brightly rain clad students.
A flag flies over the steel stick building
 waiting for its flesh.
Behind rises Hill Center, flying antennas.
Somewhere I was working in that picture,
sweat drenched t-shirt under a safety yellow plastic jacket.
Squishy gloves protecting pale soaked dead-worm hands
And the pretty lights were not pretty, just illuminating.
Allowing me to see concrete still warm from the pour
 the littered beer bottles among the piss in the corners
and my thoughts somehow afloat among the sawdust
and plastic scraps on the roof.

AIPU

Cold, barren, painted concrete block walls.

Windows that don' t open but let the cold in.

Doors that only unlock to let food pass and doctors in.

No belts, no glass, no sharps

Just your pain.

Memories carry beautiful moments,

a caress, a sigh, a whisper of love.

floating as broken glass in the night.

Cold reflecting images.

They cut. They mutilate.

'til death do us part' A promise.

Warm dripping hurt inside.

A cloying ooze that silences the shivers in cold bones:

Your Warm healing. The eyes look outward.

Senseless sky beyond locked glass.

Frozen earth, dead leaves, square cinder buildings

lifeless

Albert

The molecules, he said

I don't want to hurt them.

They say don't step on me.

The carpet can scream and die,

Can't you hear it?

The peas say don't eat me.

I can't. God said that I should take everyone's hurt on me.

I should take their pain. nobody should hurt,

He said so.

The molecules don't want me to breathe.

The room hurts, the molecules say don't hurt me.

And Albert, tell me about your kids?

I can't help them now. I'm not good.

You love them, they need you.

I 'm not good anymore. They know.

But you didn't do anything wrong.

God wants me to take everyone's pain.

He smiles, our eyes meet.

Your wife, Albert, where is she?

She knows too.

At work, the nails started screaming when he hit them.

The world talked to him.

God started telling him things.

Said it was a sin to kill yourself.

He doesn't know why God chose him to hear the molecules,

to take their pain, just that he should.

He guesses at the why.

Hey Albert, you, okay? You look asleep.

The molecules, they only whisper

When I take the pills, everything's quieter.

You okay standing up?

Huh? I 'm okay here

the molecules, he said again,

 I don't want to hurt them.

Can't you hear the carpet?

It's dinner time, come on.

I can't eat. The peas have tiny voices.

Ken at CMHC

Just sitting there and crying, twisting your hands
which are too large.
Six four on an orange plaid couch too low
and your knees too high and shaking.
Crying and forty-three years old.
Sent to this mental health center by police and court.

You scare me when you shake.
I'm afraid of your stained oxford shirt
of your grey flannel pants and square cut hair.
I'm trying to imagine why I wouldn't
beat the shit out of some fat guy
who held my son down and farted in his face.

I'm trying to stop my chest from pounding
and my hands from shaking too as you tell me.
But I don't want to hear any more of it, any of it.
I don't want to know how you found your wife had a coke
problem
and while you were working at night, she danced in clubs.
I don't want to know who she fucked or why.

Don't tell me how you found your kids in your bed that night
and her riding some fat guy and moaning in your son's bed.
Just shut up about the court giving her custody.

Please, keep to yourself your kids' stories of
Mommy with the fat guy's pee-pee in her mouth,
of sniffing powder off the kitchen floor
and your alimony and support, your house,
your cars and wife, the fat guy.
Shut up about your son's crying.
Shut up about the fat guy smacking your ex.
 Just shut the fuck up about someone farting in your kid's face.

What are we doing here?

What are we doing here listening to poetry?

Why the dark, the smoke, the stage lights?

We should be out, bodies slapping in meter,

Off rhymes of Good, and God, and Oh Gods.

Hump and squeeze with closed eyes and licking clean

like cats of chins and ears.

Can't you hear it, just out there.

Right now, they're slam-puppying and making love,

and fucking and screwing, pumping of flesh,

piston building of pleasure,

listen to the sweat drip off her nose,

getting lost, droplet, in the sheen of his body.

Can you hear the giggle as the pumping piston poots,

As the bed thumps the wall

knocking on our walls.

Come out to play, come out.

They talk better than me

They talk better than me.
I watch their words flow from mind to mouth
 to my ears where I hear the words form ideas
that live under control.
When I answer
the words stumble
on my teeth
coming out.
They lodge behind my lips
to bump and rub each other,
descending from thought.
They see me struggle,
my hands flap lamely,
 chin jutting forward,
 tongue pushing out the consonants,
 forcing language from thought
 till it flows and
 I pull back to live on
 forming lines of words, sharing
 imaginary worlds they know nothing of
 being held together inside me.

Passage of time

There's a quiet passage of time

Slow as a cat's tail flick

A feeling to life smooth as fur

Like you are being licked clean

With eyes closed, breathing slowly

What dreams run through you?

What memories wait to be lived?

You stretch your muscles

Waiting inside

Claws and teeth and heart

Why Protest?

You'd find me, the thought goes, out there
pissing on their silly heads.
Or perhaps not using my maleness
to such an advantage.
Maybe I'd just, you know, accidentally
turn on the water sprinklers
as those damn picketers chain
themselves to the clinic's door.

It isn't like I don't understand you
all wet like you are.
Believe me, I feel the not-being
of one maybe-life.
I feel it here, in my gut which ached
when I heard it was
and then wasn't.
It choked here in my throat and
stung my eyes and poofed the air around me,
so I was tossed into drowning.
I heard her cry that night
when I should have been asleep.
Do you know how a newborn's cry
can wake you from the darkest sleep.
How even as you curse, you find your legs
walking to bring you to comfort it.
Well that night after my not so loving

still technically wife informed me
that she would never forgive me for forcing her,
because I wasn't good enough,
to get rid of our second child,
that she didn't want any part of me inside of her,
and because she had to get rid of it,
that she would hate me forever, and
hugging myself and crying, not in the least able
to get out of her car after Christmas shopping
for our first born, then she said
she had felt sick and thought
the pregnancy wouldn't have been healthy anyway.
Well then, she cried and
screamed you asshole,
get out of my car.
I hadn't even known she was pregnant.
And that night the unborn, un-is cried
I couldn't go to get her, or him,
and she cried, and I tried to hold myself
to quiet the tears so I could sleep
and go to work in just three hours.

A friend you can love

A friend you can love,
even when you can't love.
It is an effortless act,
a shoulder to cry on.
Perhaps two arms to make a hug.
But there's tension between people,
of unknowing intimacy,
uncomprehending borders and stops,
that fears of not knowing.
Shared hurt or grief and fear of the pain.
Not being taken just giving.
Safe.

Stone

Pour shaped stone and steel. Branching, living,
growing from the bottom of the Hudson
and the bed rock of Harlem.
Poured fleshed over bones of iron by sullen men
in stained clothing. Roaring heart continuous of pumped air,
pressured, held and released through steel pipes,
held by men to work the stone.
Peeling back the cloth of wooden grey,
like the hands of someone stripping.
The inner shakes and crashes of debris
started and thrown down by beaten men
in and out of the bowels,
heads caught against the ceiling,
held up by swaying constructs of lines, scaffold.
Bending as they tear unthinking to expose the flesh.
Heavy fallings and the straining lifting by scurrying men inside,
rooting, rooting, and building for their lives.

7:20 am

7:20 am

New York Tuesday

From below.

"Fuck'em kid"

I hear, and gravel goes on their Guccis

With a peltering and a curse.

Electric light shadows the stacked layers

 of fill and carriage cobbles, two sand types,

grey shale and beer cans.

Survivor black cracked army boots

and the stained brown leather of mine in the mud

as we shuffle ripped glove hand opens the air

on the heavy chipper, it hisses, he smiles and slips candy

under the dust mask and scratched glasses.

You dig, shoveling at thirty stories of polished pink marble

and mirrored glass in the dawn.

He mumbles about white bread college kids.

9:00 am

"Did you see that shitty bitch?" And his gloved thumb

Points upward to thighs, a flash of white and gray flannel skirt

All with running shoes and now she's gone too.

Whistles and offers me a peanut chew that I wave off

Followed by the apricot brandy, I mumble "it's too early."

Sounds of cars again then nothing

but the sound of the chipper.

I cough dust and replace my mask to toss gravel

at the passing briefcases and blue wool.

11:30

A leaking wood steam pipe from a different time

Lies exposed and we quit for Mickey D.

Sit on a plank against the dumpster we're filling

And watch the Manhattan that was legs and brief cases

Invisible in our dirt among the dirt.

"Look at the knockers on her" and he elbows me

Whistles to the reply of "Fuck off", her eyes on me.

Big Mac wrappers blow away, more knockers pass

Followed by big boobs, blow job lips, and "hey baby"

Then a long line of bitches that "we know what they want"

3:15

Above

I pull the spark plug wire on the compressor

We both move quicker than in the morning

Planking is moved to cover our hole in Manhattan

Notes

Notes

Author information

Charles Blackwell III with C4

I had known her since the fifth grade. Back then we hardly spoke, but I noticed her in all the quiet ways a boy notices the girl who somehow feels set apart from everyone else. I admired her from a distance. Years later I learned that I had broken her school record for sit-ups in a row, a record she had been proud of, and she still teased—half seriously—that she had never quite forgiven me for it.

By our senior year of high school, I finally gathered the courage to ask her out. Being with her felt effortless and right, as if we had simply stepped into something that had always been waiting for us. We joked about how strong our feelings were, as though they might be too much for two young people just starting out in life.

Right after graduation, we faced an unexpected pregnancy. We made the difficult decision to let it go and follow our separate college plans, believing that was the responsible path. But love has a way of overruling carefully made plans. I flew to her college in Baltimore and asked her to marry me. By late September, we were husband and wife.

That December, we moved into her parents' home. I began working as a laborer in Harlem, a job arranged through a friend of my father's. I was young and determined to build something solid for us. But almost immediately, the ground beneath us began to shift.

Her mother's behavior toward me crossed boundaries in ways that left me confused, ashamed, and deeply uncomfortable. What should have been a place of support became a place of tension and fear. I felt trapped, unsure how to confront something so wrong without tearing the family apart. After months of carrying it alone, I finally told my wife. Instead of relief, I felt distance grow between us. A week later, she asked me to move out, saying everything had become too overwhelming.

The following August, after saving every dollar I could, I secured an apartment for us. We moved in together with our son. I was exhausted but hopeful. I could take college classes, work hard, and move us toward the future I imagined.

For a time, I believed things were stabilizing. Then, during spring finals, she told me she couldn't continue like this and left, leaving our son. Two weeks later she returned, demanding the apartment deposit and saying her parents would raise our son while she focused on school. I was desperate to comply, to do whatever it took to hold our family together.

In trying to recover that deposit, I found myself exploited again—this time by someone who offered help but instead violated my trust and dignity. I left that encounter shaken and numb, carrying yet another secret shame.

Even after the money was returned, she would not speak to me. She said she couldn't be a mother, a wife, and a student all at once. If I waited patiently and didn't upset her, she promised, everything would eventually work out. I clung to those words. A year later, while exchanging our son for babysitting, she told me she still loved me. A few months after that, we were in a new apartment, trying again. I never stopped loving her. I wanted nothing more than for us to be a family.

Then she suffered a car accident that left her unconscious and struggling afterward with memory and focus. She would call me in tears, unable to find her classes. Around the same time, I lost my job as a carpenter and had to borrow money from my parents to cover rent. We were both fragile, frightened of what the future held.

A neurologist warned us that many marriages do not survive that kind of brain injury and urged counseling. Terrified of losing her, I told her how afraid I was. She assured me that the past year had been the happiest of her life and insisted we would be fine. To comfort me, she wrote a three-page letter for me to keep—something to show her if she ever forgot that she loved me.

The first page listed the ways she felt I had hurt her and how she had forgiven each one. The second page described everything she cherished about our life together. The third page was filled with her hopes for our future. She cried as she handed it to me. I held that letter like a promise. She later shared a class with an acquaintance of mine. Wanting to support her studies, I asked him to help her. I trusted them both.

One day, after visiting my union hall in Harlem to look for work, I ran into mutual friends who offered condolences for a divorce I knew nothing about. They told me that this man had been publicly boasting about being with my wife, speaking of her in crude and humiliating ways, reducing her to stories and insults about her scars, stretch marks and saggy breasts, never even using her name—only calling her "Charlie's ex."

I went home in disbelief and quietly tried to verify what I'd heard. I couldn't bring myself to accuse her outright. I only asked that she stop studying with him. When she refused, something inside me broke. Depression settled over me like a fog. I couldn't eat alone. I cried constantly. I felt as if the world I had fought so hard to build was collapsing. She told me to find work by the end of the month or she would leave. I found three jobs in quick succession—waitering on weekends, security at night, carpentry again during the day—terrified that any failure would cost me my family. I told myself the affair, if it was real, might pass. That we could still heal.

Then one evening I came home to an empty apartment. She was gone. Our son was gone. My world fell silent.

When I showed her the letter she had written—the one she had wept over—she denied ever writing it. She called it fake and threatened me for bringing it up. I felt as though reality itself had been erased.

The divorce process was brutal. She accused me of stalking her, and visitation with my son was cut off for four months until our court date. In court she admitted there had been no stalking, and the judge reprimanded her for exploiting his concern for women in genuine danger.

A court-appointed therapist recommended that I receive primary custody, stating that she struggled to see our son's needs as separate from her own. A second psychologist, after six visits, reached the same conclusion. A third evaluation was requested. My attorney quietly told me that the judge would be unlikely to grant me custody under almost any circumstances. The third psychologist recommended split custody with generous visitation for me, which allowed the judge to order the standard alternate-weekend arrangement despite the earlier recommendations.

Through it all, what remained constant was my love for my son and my enduring grief over the woman I had known since childhood—the girl I had admired from afar, the young woman I had flown across states to marry, the mother of my child. I had held onto hope again and again, believing love and persistence would be enough. In the end, I was left carrying the pieces: the memories, the letter she said never existed, and the quiet determination to remain present for my son, even when the life I imagined had slipped beyond my reach.

www.ingramcontent.com/pod-product-compliance
Lightning Source LLC
Chambersburg PA
CBHW070645030426

42337CB00020B/4167